101 FREAKY ANIMALS

ISBN 978-0-545-23758-1

10 9 8 7 6 5 4   11 12 13 14

Printed in the U.S.A.   40
First printing, September 2010
Book design by Kay Petronio

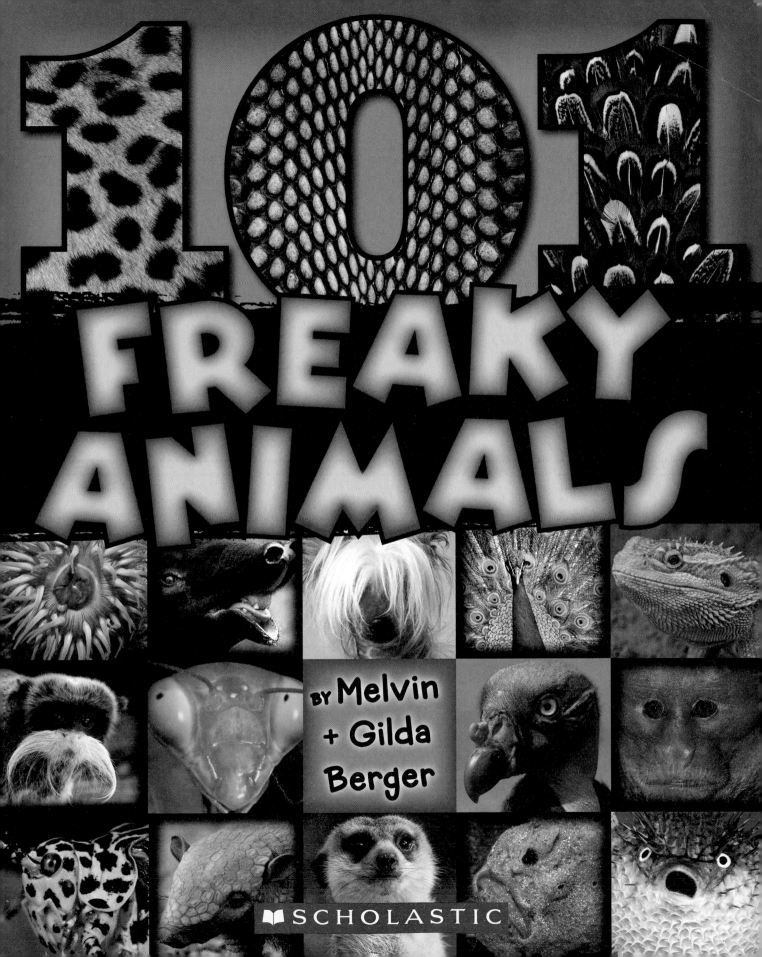

101 FREAKY ANIMALS

BY Melvin + Gilda Berger

SCHOLASTIC

Aardvarks are mammals that live in Africa. An aardvark's favorite foods are ants and termites, which it catches with its long, sticky tongue. When in danger, an aardvark uses its front paws like a shovel to escape enemies, such as lions or leopards. Digging fast, the aardvark makes a deep hole—and down it goes.

#1 AARDVARKS HAVE PAWS LIKE SHOVELS

#2 ANGLER FISH LIGHT UP

The female angler fish has a kind of fishing pole on top of her head. At the end of the pole is a small, glowing blob, called an esca. The fish brings the esca down in front of her mouth. Fish passing by come close for a better look. The sly angler fish whips the esca away and opens her huge mouth. Then her long, pointed teeth slam shut on the prey.

Armadillos are small mammals with hard shells of bony plates called carapaces. These shells are like heavy suits of armor. They are an armadillo's best protection against predators. The three-banded armadillo is even better protected. When attacked, this armadillo curls itself up into a hard, tight ball. Few enemies can grasp the curled-up armadillo with their teeth or claws.

#3 ARMADILLOS WEAR ARMOR

#4 AXOLOTLS NEVER BECOME ADULTS

Axolotls may look like fish, but they are not fish at all! They are amphibians, like frogs are. Axolotls are larvae, similar to the tadpole stage in a frog's life cycle. Like some kinds of newts and salamanders, axolotls never change into adults. They breathe through gills as long as they live. Although they have fins, they actually walk in the water.

Aye-ayes hunt at night. Their main food is insects from the forests of Madagascar. Like woodpeckers, aye-ayes tap on trees to find their food. The difference is that aye-ayes tap with their long, thin third finger. Dull thuds tell them there are insects inside. Then they gnaw a hole in the wood, poke in a finger, and pull out their dinner.

#5 AYE-AYES TAP TREES TO FIND FOOD

#6 BABIRUSAS ARE PIGS WITH TUSKS

Babirusas are wild pigs found on the tropical islands of Indonesia. Unlike other pigs, males grow tusks from their upper and lower jaws. During mating season, the males fight other males to win the females. The male babirusas stand up on their rear legs and jab upward with their two sharp lower tusks.

Bearded dragons' "beards" are folds of loose skin with spiky scales that hang under their lower jaws. These lizards can make their beards larger. Males mostly use their expanded beards to attract females. Females use their beards to frighten enemies. After two male bearded dragons fight, the loser stands on three legs and slowly waves a forelimb. This act says that he gives up.

#7 BEARDED DRAGONS HAVE "BEARDS" OF SKIN

BIRDS OF PARADISE #8 SHOW OFF THEIR FEATHERS

Most adult male birds of paradise are brightly colored. And they have extra-long feathers under their wings. To get a mate, the male spreads out his feathers like a huge, open fan. He sways, spins, twirls, and does other dance steps that show off his amazing feathers. Some males even hang upside down to win their lady's attention.

Blue-tongued skinks are like other lizards. They are covered with scales and tend to be gray or brown. They prey on insects and other small animals. But when attacked, blue-tongued skinks are not like other lizards. Skinks open their bright pink mouths, hiss loudly, and stick out their blue tongues. Who wouldn't be scared by such a sight?

#9 BLUE-TONGUED SKINKS STICK OUT THEIR TONGUES

#10 BOOMSLANG SNAKES HAVE FREAKY FANGS

Boomslangs have fangs way back in their jaws. This is different from most poisonous snakes, which have fangs at the front of their mouths. When it attacks, the boomslang snake injects poison, or venom, into its prey. The venom takes a long time to act. But once it does, it is deadly.

Brush-snouted weevils are beetles with long, bushy snouts. Some snouts are even longer than the rest of the body. The snout has a tiny set of jaws at the hairy tip. The snout is not very attractive. But it is the perfect tool for the weevil to use when digging into tree bark to find food for its young or to lay eggs.

#11 BRUSH-SNOUTED WEEVILS HAVE LONG SNOUTS

#12 BUSH BABIES CRY

The bush baby gets its name both from its cries and from its small size. This odd forest animal comes out mostly at night. Large eyes and amazingly sharp hearing help it find insects and other food in the dark. At the end of the night, bush babies cry out to one another, sounding like human babies. Then they gather together to sleep in nests of leaves or in tree holes.

Capybaras are South American relatives of mice—but they are about 16 times the size of mice and 1,600 times as heavy. They are often called water pigs because of their great size. Capybaras live near lakes and rivers, where they eat grass that grows on the land and weeds that grow in the water.

#13 CAPYBARAS ARE GIANT RODENTS

#14 CASSOWARIES LOOK DRESSED UP

The cassowary looks dressed up all the time. Two long, crazy-colored folds of skin, or wattles, hang from its neck. Some say this flashy getup helps these birds find mates. Others believe it lets them find one another in the dark forests where they live. But the daggerlike claws mean only one thing: The cassowary is fit for fighting.

Chinese crested dogs probably won't win a cutest dog contest. While some have a few hairs on their heads, many are born hairless. Their skin feels very much like yours does and can be any color from pale white to black. But what can we say about their huge red tongues? No one knows why they're so big and red.

#15 CHINESE CRESTED DOGS TAKE THE PRIZE

#16 CRESTED NEWTS HAVE CROWNS OF GILLS

The crested newt is an amphibian that spends part of its life in water and part on land. When it is young, a crested newt has four frilly "feathers" sticking out of its head. These "feathers" are really gills. They let young newts breathe underwater. As the newts become adults, the gills disappear and lungs develop. Once they develop lungs, the newts can breathe air and live on land—but they lose their crowns!

The crowned crane is named for its headdress of stiff golden feathers. But the headdress has nothing to do with the way it calls, or honks. To do this, the bird uses the bright red throat pouch that hangs beneath its face. The crane puffs up the sac with air. Then it opens its beak and gives an eerie *honk!* that can be heard from quite a distance.

17 CROWNED CRANES HONK LOUDLY

#18 CUTTLEFISH AREN'T FISH

Cuttlefish are more like squid and octopuses than they are like fish. Their W-shaped eyes are very unusual. But so are their eight short arms and two long tentacles, which are used to capture prey. Oddest of all is their ability to change skin color quickly. A cuttlefish can switch from brown to yellow, red, black, or a mix of colors in a matter of seconds.

Most crabs are covered by hard shells. But the bodies of decorator crabs are covered with tiny hooked bristles. As these crabs move through the water, they hang bits of seaweed or other material on the hooks. Once their bodies are covered, decorator crabs can hide from their enemies on the ocean floor. Even humans find them hard to see.

#19 DECORATOR CRABS USE SEAWEED TO HIDE

DUGONG SNOUTS FACE DOWN

20

The dugong lives in shallow, warm waters and grazes on plants growing there. The animal's funny snout—with the mouth on the bottom—is the perfect shape for eating sea grass, a dugong's main food. It uses its thick lips to grasp the plants and pull them up. For that reason, dugongs are called sea cows.

Echidnas are plump, spiny mammals that live in Australia and New Zealand. They are among the very few mammals that lay eggs. They also have no teeth. Since they are toothless, how do they chew ants, their main food? Echidnas mash them with spiked plates in their mouths. Then they swallow the soft mush.

#21 ECHIDNAS ARE TOOTHLESS WONDERS

#22 ELEPHANT SHREWS ARE VERY NOSY

Elephant shrews have excellent sight and hearing. But their sense of smell is even better. The elephant shrew's long nose is always twitching—moving from side to side. The constant movement helps the shrew sniff out bugs and other food on the forest floor. With elephant shrews, the nose knows everything!

The most wacky feature of the emperor tamarin is its long, drooping white mustache. This monkey lives in the tropical forests of South America. Its name comes from the similar mustache of the former German emperor Wilhelm II. The tamarin's mustache, however, is even longer. It reaches down below the tamarin's shoulders.

#23 EMPEROR TAMARINS SPROUT MUSTACHES

FENNEC FOXES

#24 GROW HUGE EARS

The ears of the fennec fox are almost half as long as its body. Can you guess why? Big ears help the fennec fox hear prey at night in the Sahara Desert where it lives. The fox can even pick up the sounds of insects, rodents, and lizards hiding underground. Also, the ears' large surface helps rid the body of heat and keep it cool.

You can tell the flannel moth caterpillar by its thick, hairy cover. Some of the hairs, or spines, are soft and harmless. But many are hard, hollow, and filled with poison. When these spines break off in someone's skin, they burn and sting. At worst, they cause pain and even paralysis. So watch out for these very hairy, eerie bugs!

#25 FLANNEL MOTH CATERPILLARS ARE VERY HAIRY

#26 FLOUNDER HAVE CROOKED FACES

A newborn flounder has an eye on each side of its face. But as the fish grows, one eye slowly moves toward the other eye. In time, both eyes are on the same side of its head. The mouth doesn't move, though, which is how the fish gets a crooked face. Flounder lie flat on the seafloor, with both eyes looking up. This keeps them safe from enemies while they catch shrimp and small fish to eat.

A flying squirrel has folds of furry skin on each side of its body. The skin connects the front and back legs to form two wings. The wings let the squirrel glide from tree to tree in thick forests. A single glide of the southern flying squirrel can be about 100 yards (91.4 m)—the length of a football field! Their flat tails act like brakes that help them slow down before they land.

#27 FLYING SQUIRRELS GLIDE BETWEEN TREES

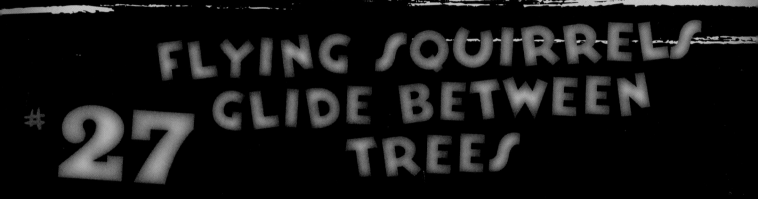

#28 FRILLED LIZARDS ARE SCARY BUT HARMLESS

The frilled lizard of Australia has a few ways to keep safe. When threatened by an eagle, owl, or snake, this lizard runs for its life. But if a predator gets too close, the lizard suddenly stops, opens its mouth wide, and spreads out the brightly colored frill around its neck. If all else fails to scare away the enemy, the lizard lets out a scary—but harmless—*hiss!*

Frogfish lie on the muddy ocean bottom, waiting for their prey. Eventually, a small sea creature swims or drifts by. The frogfish stretches out a small, wormlike white lure that hangs down from its head. Thinking the lure is food, the creature tries to catch it. The waiting frogfish slams its jaws shut—and captures its meal.

#29 FROGFISH HUNT WITH LURES

#30 GARDEN EELS LIVE IN BURROWS

Garden eels make their homes in burrows on the sandy bottom of the ocean. Thousands live together, like flowers in a garden. These "gardens" of eels sway in the water, feeding on tiny sea creatures drifting by. If frightened, the eels use their powerful tails to dig deeper holes into the sand. What great hiding places!

Ghost crabs spend most of their time in sandy burrows on ocean beaches. With two black eyes atop their heads like periscopes, they look all around for sand fleas or other little animals to eat. Ghost crabs take their name from their clear bodies, which make them hard to see on sand. When threatened, they disappear down burrows at lightning speeds.

#31 GHOST CRABS TURN THEIR EYES IN EVERY DIRECTION

#32 GIANT ANTEATERS HAVE TINY MOUTHS

Giant anteaters, as you might guess, mostly eat ants. Their snouts can be 2 feet (0.6 m) long. But their mouths are only about the size of a penny, which is the perfect size to trap ants inside. The anteater eats some 30,000 ants each day. It has sharp, curved claws for tearing open ants' nests and a long, thin, sticky tongue to lick up the insects.

Giant clams are the biggest shellfish in the world. These huge sea creatures are large enough for an average second grader to fit inside! People used to think giant clams could snap their shells shut on divers' arms or legs. But now we know that clams shut their shells very slowly—and only to protect themselves.

#33 GIANT CLAMS ARE MONSTER SHELLFISH

GIRAFFE WEEVILS HAVE L-O-N-G NECKS
#34

Giraffe weevils have very long necks, which they put to good use. They stretch them out to eat the leaves of some small trees. The male sometimes uses his longer neck to roll leaves into little tubes. The female lays a single egg inside each one. When the eggs hatch, the newborns eat the leaves they were rolled in.

Most people know that giraffes are the tallest animals. But few know that giraffes also have the roughest, toughest tongues. The giraffe's favorite food is the leaves of the thorny acacia tree. It uses its very long, thick tongue to reach around the thorns and pull the leaves off the branches. Its syrupy saliva helps protect the tongue and coat any thorns it might swallow.

#35 GIRAFFES ARE TOUGH-TONGUED

#36 GOLDEN SNUB-NOSED MONKEYS LOOK SNOOTY

Golden snub-nosed monkeys get their name from the way their short noses turn up at the end. Some think it makes them look stuck-up. But that is not their only freaky feature. Their round mouths are white and hairless, and their bright eyes are circled in blue. They have coats of reddish fur to keep them warm in their cold mountain homes.

Great diving beetles live in freshwater ponds and streams. They use smell, touch, and sight to hunt their prey underwater. With their very strong mouth parts, the beetles grab, stab, and tear apart their prey. Great diving beetles are called water tigers because of their huge appetites. Their favorite prey ranges widely, from small fish to tadpoles. Some have even been known to eat full-grown frogs!

#37 GREAT DIVING BEETLES HAVE BIG APPETITES

#38 GREAT INDIAN HORNBILLS BATTLE IT OUT

The great Indian hornbill has a huge bill topped with a very large, horny growth, or casque. The bill looks heavy, even though it is hollow and as light as a sponge. Males use their casques as weapons in midair fights with other males. The casque also makes their calls in the rain forest loud and harsh.

Green iguanas are large lizards that live in tropical forests. Unlike most other lizards, the green iguana has a tiny third "eye" on the top of its head. This "eye" sees movement and changes in light and dark, which warn of enemies in the trees above. The two main eyes let the iguana spot insects and other prey.

#39 GREEN IGUANAS HAVE THREE EYES

#40 GULPER EELS CAN SWALLOW HUGE FISH

Gulper eels live in very deep, dark ocean water. The hungry eel swims along slowly with its huge mouth wide open. Big and little fish wash in, along with lots of water. The eel shuts its mouth, squeezes out the water, and swallows the fish left behind. Since its mouth stretches so wide, a gulper eel can swallow fish larger than its body.

Hagfish are sometimes caught by bigger sea creatures. To escape, the hagfish oozes a thick slime. This slime makes the hagfish slippery and hard to hold. The predator lets go and the hagfish escapes. Later, it gets rid of the slime in a cool way. It forms its body into a knot and slides the knot down, head to tail, pushing the slime off its body. Imagine that!

#41 HAGFISH ESCAPE WITH SLIME

#42 HAMMERHEAD SHARKS LOOK LIKE HAMMERS

A hammerhead shark has eyes at the ends of its hammer-shaped head. Strange as this is, the shark uses its head wisely. The shark's head helps propel its body as it swims and hunts in the sea. Its widely spaced eyes help it find stingrays and other food. The sides of the head also hold the rays in the sand while the shark feeds hungrily.

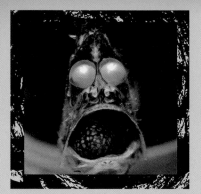

Hatchet fish swim near the bottom of the sea. They have two monster eyes that face up to see the fish swimming above them. A hatchet fish attacks suddenly from below. It nabs the prey in its upturned mouth. Meanwhile, the hatchet fish dims or brightens the lights on its body to blend in with the light from above. This helps it hide from predators even deeper in the sea.

#43 HATCHET FISH EYES FACE UP

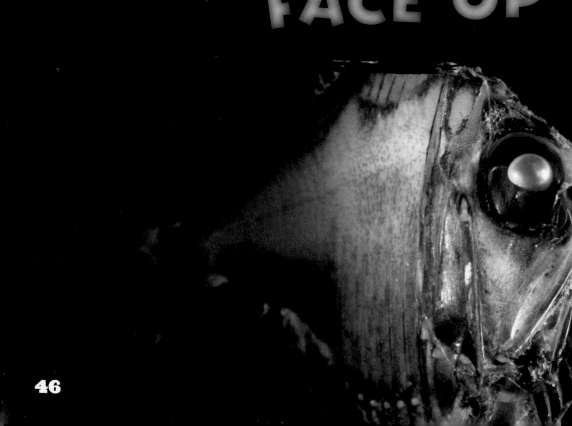

#44 HOATZINS SMELL BAD

Hoatzins of South America are foul-smelling birds. Scientists think they know why. Hoatzins eat leaves that they pull off trees. They roll the leaves into balls and stuff them into their mouths. As part of the digestive process, the balls stay in the body so long that germs ferment, or sour. The birds get very smelly. For this reason, hoatzins are nicknamed stink birds.

A hooded seal has a flap of skin hanging down in front of its upper lip. What happens if a male seal grows angry, frightened, or excited, or wants to impress a female? The male quickly blows up the flap. It forms a red balloon that is about twice as big as a football. Watch out! A fight may be about to start.

#45 HOODED SEALS BLOW UP

#46 HORSESHOE CRABS HAVE SPIKELIKE TAILS

Horseshoe crabs have been around since before the dinosaurs. They have not changed in 445 million years. Horseshoe crabs are actually more closely related to spiders and scorpions than to crabs. A long, spikelike tail helps the horseshoe crab steer in the water and flip over should it land on its back.

A jellyfish has no brain, head, bones, skin, or blood! Its body is filled with a jellylike substance, from which it gets its name. Long strings, called tentacles, hang down from its body. Each has thousands of stingers that can shoot poison into any creature it touches. The poison usually paralyzes or kills the prey.

#47 JELLYFISH CAN BE DEADLY

#48 KATYDIDS ONLY SING AT NIGHT

Katydids are large green grasshoppers that live in trees and are only active at night. The call of the males sounds like they are singing "katydid, katy-didn't" on late summer or autumn evenings. They keep making these shrill sounds all through the night. When other male katydids hear the song from nearby trees, they join in. Soon the air is filled with a chorus of these insects singing "katydid, katy-didn't" all night long.

King vultures are colorful birds that eat dead animals. They live in the rain forests of Central and South America. Feathers cover their bodies, but their heads and necks are bare. Bald upper parts help king vultures stay healthy. If they weren't bald, rotting meat might stick to their feathers after each bloody meal and make them ill.

#49 KING VULTURES ARE BALD

KIWIS FIND FOOD THEY CAN'T
#50 SEE OR FEEL

Kiwis are New Zealand birds that cannot fly. They depend on an exceptional sense of smell to find food they cannot actually see. This is a most unusual trait in birds. In fact, kiwis are the only birds with nostrils at the end of their long beaks. They can pick up the slightest odors of the fruits, insects, and worms they feed on—even those hidden under the ground.

Komodo dragons have very weak eyes and poor hearing. But their snakelike forked tongues let them smell their food, such as pigs and small deer, from far away. The Komodo dragon lies in wait for its prey. Then it uses its sharp claws and teeth to attack the animal's feet, knocking it to the ground. The dragon holds its prey while injecting it with venom. As the victim grows weak, the dragon starts to eat.

#51 KOMODO DRAGONS SMELL WITH THEIR TONGUES

#52 KOMONDOR DOGS HAVE A WEIRD HAIRSTYLE

A komondor dog's hair is long, thick, and ropelike. The bulky cords of their coats hang down and drag along the ground. Perhaps their fur is heavy because komondors were originally used as sheep dogs. They were bred to have heavy coats to protect them against wolves or other predators.

The long, upward-facing nose of a lantern bug is really its stretched-out mouth, called a proboscis. But lantern bugs don't use their large mouths for biting. Instead, they use it to suck the sap, or juice, from flowers and trees. Although they are called lantern bugs, they do not give off light. Their bright wings just reflect light and look like they are glowing.

#53 LANTERN BUGS' NOSES POINT UP

#54 LEAFY SEA DRAGONS LOOK LIKE SEAWEED

Leafy sea dragons do not look like other fish. The green, orange, and gold of their bodies match the colors of the seaweed in the water. Also, the jagged shapes of their fins make them look more like plants in the sea. Since they can easily blend in with their surroundings, a predator looking for a meal does not notice them. Only the fluttering of their tiny fins gives them away.

The lionfish protects itself with sharp spines that sting. Each spine is like a thin, pointed needle that injects poison into any animal that frightens the lionfish. Someone that steps on the spines also gets a very painful—but not deadly—sting. Part of the lionfish's scientific name is Greek for "wasp," because of its sting.

#55 LIONFISH STING LIKE WASPS

#56 LORISES' EYES ARE SAUCERLIKE

Lorises are like other monkeys in many ways, but they have no tails. One kind, known as the slender loris, is about the size of a chipmunk. This loris lives in forests and comes out at night to find the smelly insects and other food it feeds on. Two huge eyes help it spot its food in the dark. Good sight also helps the loris make its way quietly through the branches without alerting its prey.

Male mandrills are the most brightly colored of all mammals. Their faces and bottoms have similar striking colors. These bizarre looks have an important purpose. The colors are easy to see in the thick forests where the monkeys live. This helps groups of mandrills stay together as they move along the ground or through the trees.

MANDRILLS' FACES ARE RED, WHITE, AND BLUE

#57

MANED WOLVES LOOK LIKE ANIMALS ON STILTS

#58

For some two million years, maned wolves, which have very long legs, have lived on South American grasslands. These open areas are covered with very tall grass. Long-legged wolves were able to get over the grass more easily and find more food than wolves with short legs. The long-legged ones survived, while the other wolves died out.

A manta ray is about as wide as a soccer goal. It weighs more than some cars do. Yet it leaps gracefully out of the water. Its main food is plankton, which is made up of tiny animals and plants that float in the water. The manta ray also eats very small shrimp and fish. It takes huge amounts of these little bits of food to fill its big stomach.

MANTA RAYS EAT NOTHING LARGER THAN SHRIMP

#59

#60 MATA MATA TURTLES ARE TRICKY

Mata mata turtles live in shallow, slow-moving streams or swamps. Their triangular heads and bumpy shells look like leaves or bark that fell into the water. This disguise helps the turtle hide in its wet surroundings. But a fish that comes close had better watch out. The mata mata can suddenly suck it in and gulp it down.

Meerkats are four-legged animals that eat insects, lizards, snakes, and other small animals. But while some hunt for food, other meerkats stand guard on two legs, watching for predators. Looking almost human, they balance themselves with their long, thin tails. Those standing guard peep when all is well and bark or whistle if they spot danger.

#61 MEERKATS STAND GUARD ON TWO LEGS

#62 MUDSKIPPERS SWIM AND WALK

Mudskippers are fish that live along ocean coasts. When the tide is in, they use their fins to swim in the ocean. They breathe through their gills. When the tide goes out, the mudskippers stay on the muddy land. They walk and jump around on their fins. And they breathe through their skin—until the tide comes back in.

Naked mole rats are wrinkled animals with little hair. But they are neither moles nor rats. Their closest relatives are porcupines! Naked mole rats live in vast tunnel systems that they dig with their huge front teeth. Lucky for them, their teeth are in front of their lips—so they don't get dirt in their mouths.

#63 NAKED MOLE RATS LIVE UNDERGROUND

#64 NARWHALS GROW TUSKS

Narwhals are whales from the Arctic with only two teeth. In males, one tooth grows unusually twisted and long. It becomes a heavy tusk that sticks straight out of the whale's head. Scientists believe that the male with the longest tusk becomes the leader of the pod, or group.

Octopuses have a bagful of tricks to escape predators. They can flee by squirting water out of their bodies and jetting away at high speed. They can change their skin color so they are hard to see. They can spread dark ink in the water to confuse attackers. And they can escape predators by squeezing through tiny openings in rocks or caves.

#65 OCTOPUSES ARE ESCAPE ARTISTS

OKAPIS WASH WITH THEIR TONGUES

#66

The okapi's foot-long (30 cm) tongue helps it reach for leaves high in a tree. It also helps the okapi keep clean. Okapis can stretch their tongues far enough around to wash their eyes and ears. And what about the zebralike stripes on their legs? They help camouflage okapis in the African rain forests where they live.

The pangolin is the only mammal with scales. The scales are the same material as your fingernails—but much harder. When in danger, the pangolin sticks its head between its front legs. It can even curl into a ball, tucking its head under its tail to protect itself. To clean its body, the pangolin lifts the scales with its legs or tongue and reaches underneath.

#67 PANGOLINS ARE MAMMALS WITH SCALES

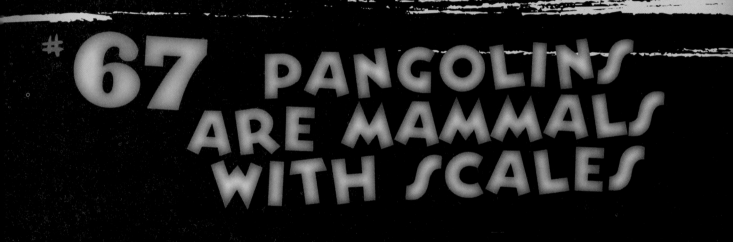

#68 PEACOCKS SHOW OFF

Peacocks (male peafowl) are the biggest show-offs of all birds. They drag behind them long trains of greenish feathers dotted with spots that look like eyes. When trying to attract a female, the peacock spreads out his amazing feathers. He shivers and shakes to make the colors look even better. Few females can ignore this stunning display.

Pig-nosed turtles take their name from the piggy shape of their snouts. They live in lakes and rivers and use their snouts to breathe underwater. These turtles differ from other freshwater turtles in two main ways. Their front limbs are shaped like paddles and their back legs have webbed toes. Both features help them swim swiftly through the water while they look for food.

#69 PIG-NOSED TURTLES SWIM SWIFTLY

#70 PLATYPUSES HAVE DUCK BILLS

The platypus is said to be one of the freakiest animals of all. It has a duck's bill, a mole's fur, a beaver's tail, and an otter's webbed feet! But of all its strange parts, its flat bill is the most peculiar. The platypus uses it to feel and scoop up tiny animals from the river bottom. Then it comes ashore to grind up its meal with the hard ridges in its bill.

Porcupine fish look like other fish until attacked. Then they gulp in huge amounts of water or air and blow themselves up to three times their usual size. They become as big and round as soccer balls. Their spines, which usually lie flat, pop up like a porcupine's quills. This can scare away even the fiercest attackers.

#71 PORCUPINE FISH PUFF UP

#72 PRAYING MANTISES' LEGS LOOK LIKE HANDS

The praying mantis gets its name from the way it folds its front legs. The legs look like hands folded in prayer. But looks are deceiving. The praying mantis is just waiting to strike. Any kind of insect, even those of its own kind, had better watch out. The praying mantis shoots out its forelegs to catch its prey. Then their sharp hooks hold the victim tightly while the praying mantis gobbles it up.

Proboscis monkeys make their forest homes only on the island of Borneo. They have super big noses that face downward. The female's nose is smaller than that of the male. But the male's huge nose is important. When the male calls out to a female, his nose makes the sound louder. The nose also boosts the sound of honks that warn others of danger.

#73 PROBOSCIS MONKEYS HAVE MONSTROUS NOSES

RED CROSSBILLS HAVE CRISSCROSSED BILLS

#74

Red crossbills have special bills that cross at the tip. The birds use their bills to pry open cones such as pinecones. Inside they find the seeds that are their main food. Crossbills start at the bottom of a cone and spiral upward. They open each scale and remove the seeds with their tongues. Some of these birds have bills crossed to the right, some to the left.

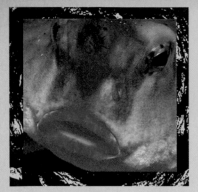

The red-lipped batfish is found in the tropical Pacific Ocean off the coasts of Central and South America. It has two big, showy, ruby red lips that give it its name. This fish spends most of its time on the ocean floor, collecting shellfish, small fish, and worms. A poor swimmer, the batfish uses its fins like feet for walking. A strange horn on its head hides a fishing pole, like the one on an angler fish.

RED-LIPPED BATFISH HAVE RUBY LIPS

#75

#76 ROBBER FLIES CATCH PREY IN MIDAIR

Robber flies look fearsome. They have stout, spiny legs, two large compound eyes, and a bristly mustache. The robber fly catches insects for food in midair. Then it injects the prey with poisonous saliva. The saliva digests the bugs' insides, which the robber fly sucks up. Lucky for us, they don't harm humans.

Scorpions do not only look scary, they're also deadly. Their bodies are little killing machines for large insects and spiders. The front pair of clawed pincers captures the prey. Then the rest of the body either crushes the animal or injects it with poison. The scorpion's poison comes from a curved stinger at the tip of its tail. *Sting!* The prey is paralyzed or killed.

#77 SCORPIONS HAVE KILLER STINGERS

#78 SEA ANEMONES LOOK LIKE FLOWERS

The sea anemone is a peculiar sea creature. It looks like a flower but is really a small animal. It can move slowly, but one end usually stays fixed to a rock, coral reef, or shell. The other end has a mouth surrounded by tiny arms, or tentacles, that wave in the water. The tentacles sting small creatures passing by, which the anemone slips into its mouth.

Sea cucumbers look like anything but what they are—animals that live on the ocean floor. They crawl on feet covered with hundreds of tiny suction cups. Their bumpy skin helps hide them from predators. Frightened sea cucumbers shoot out their insides to confuse predators. They leave their organs behind and new ones grow back in a few weeks.

#79 SEA CUCUMBERS SHOOT OUT THEIR INSIDES

#80 SEA HORSES HAVE A GRASPING TAIL

Sea horses have the heads of tiny horses, which give them their name. This fish is the only one with a long, grasping tail. It coils the tail around plants growing in the sea to anchor itself. Then it sucks small sea creatures into the end of its long snout. The male sea horse is a good father. He carries the female's eggs in his pouch until they hatch.

The sea urchin has no brain, yet it survives very well in its deep-sea home. Sea urchins have sharp spines that stick out from the skin of their round bodies. They feed on waste matter that drifts down to the sea bottom. But they also chew seaweed and living animals that they find on rocks. The mouth, with five sharp teeth, is a tiny hole on the urchin's underside.

#81 SEA URCHINS ARE BRAINLESS

#82 SHOEBILLS HAVE ENORMOUS BEAKS

The shoebill is a large wading bird that lives in African swamps and marshes. It has the largest bill, or beak, of any bird. The bird needs its bill to grab the fish and other large, slippery prey it eats. Its shoelike bill is so big and heavy that it points down. The shoebill lays the huge bill on its chest when it is resting.

Shovel-nosed frogs live on the muddy banks of ponds in Africa. Their hard-tipped, pointy snouts are perfect tools for digging headfirst in the mud. Like shovels, the noses push away the soil as the frogs tunnel for earthworms and termites to feed on. Their powerful hind legs help them dig, not jump.

#83 SHOVEL-NOSED FROGS DIG WITH THEIR NOSES

#84 SPHYNX CATS HAVE NO FUR

Sphynx cats are called hairless, or bald, because they have no fur. Their bodies are covered with soft fuzz, like peaches. Though they are called sphynx cats, they are not Egyptian. The first ones were born in Canada in 1966. Since then, these curious, much-loved cats have become popular household pets.

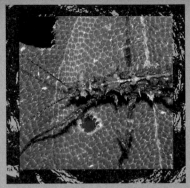

Spiny stick insects fool predators—and they could probably fool you. That's because they look just like sticks with dead leaves on them. Their legs are covered with flat, ragged, leaflike growths. When disturbed, they sway from side to side to mimic leaves in a breeze. The females are twice as big as the males, and they live three times as long.

#85 SPINY STICK INSECTS SWAY LIKE LEAVES

#86 SQUIRREL MONKEYS LEAP FROM TREE TO TREE

Squirrel monkeys leap among the treetops to find insects on leaves. These little gymnasts also fling themselves from tree to tree—even with young on their backs. Their long tails make good balancing poles that keep them from falling. When resting, the monkeys often curl their tails over one shoulder. How cool is that?

Stag beetles have jaws like antlers. Males use these large, powerful mouth parts to fight other males and win the best mates. As larvae, these fearsome-looking insects feed on rotting wood and roots. They are harmless to humans, but sometimes they nip or pinch. This has earned them the nickname pinching bugs.

#87 STAG BEETLES PINCH

#88 STAR-NOSED MOLES TOUCH TO "SEE"

A star-nosed mole has the best sense of touch of any mammal. The reason is the 22 tentacles, or "fingers," at the tip of its nose. Since the moles are almost blind and deaf, they must depend on touch to find food. They dig shallow tunnels in the North American wetlands where they live. Then they use their noses to find worms and bugs.

Stinkbugs are insects with special glands near their stomachs. When threatened, the stinkbug opens its glands and gives off a rotten-smelling liquid. Most enemies take one whiff and leave. Some bite the stinkbug and find that it tastes as bad as it smells. They quickly spit it out. Others don't seem to mind the taste at all.

#89 STINKBUGS SPRAY BAD ODORS

#90 STONEFISH ARE POISONOUS

The stonefish is one of the most poisonous fish in the world. It lives in the tropical parts of the Pacific and Indian oceans. Usually hard to see, it lies still on the ocean floor. More than a dozen long, sharp, poisonous spines stick up from its back. Beware. Each spine forces poison out of its tip, causing pain and even death.

Surinam toads live in the waters around South America. The females lay their eggs while doing somersaults in the water. The males then press the eggs into the females' thick, spongy backs. Ten weeks later, the eggs hatch. Small toads pop out and swim away—with no help from their parents.

#91 SURINAM TOADS ARE STRANGE PARENTS

TAPIRS HAVE POINTED HEADS

#92

Tapirs look like pigs and elephants, but they are more like horses and rhinoceroses. A tapir has a short, movable trunk formed by its nose and upper lip. With this small trunk, tapirs can sniff out and touch the tropical plants they eat. Pointed heads help them move faster and more easily through thick forest undergrowth.

Tarantulas are the world's largest spiders. Their bodies are covered with short, spearlike hairs that tarantulas can use to defend themselves against their would-be predators. When a tarantula catches a bird, lizard, or other small animal, it knocks it down with its front legs. Then it gives it a poisonous bite. The poison turns the prey's body to mush, which the tarantula sucks up.

#93 TARANTULAS ARE HAIRY AND SCARY

#94 TARSIERS HAVE STARTLING EYES

Tarsiers have the most enormous eyes. Each eyeball is bigger than the tarsier's brain or stomach! A tarsier's eyes cannot move, but the animal can turn its head in almost all directions. Big eyes help the tarsier hunt at night. In fact, the bigger the eyes, the better they see. Tarsiers catch insects and even birds by jumping up and catching them in flight.

Temminck's tragopans mainly live in the thick mountain forests of China. Males have a pair of horns on their heads. Their dazzling bibs are usually hidden. But in the spring, the males show off for the females. They inflate their horns and spread their bright red and blue bibs. What a sight to see!

#95 TEMMINCK'S TRAGOPANS INFLATE THEIR HORNS

#96 THORNY DEVILS ARE HARD TO SWALLOW

Thorny devils take their name from the two sharp spikes on their head. They are also covered with pointed spines to stop enemies from trying to swallow them. Thorny devils live in the dry deserts of Australia and are often thirsty. They get water in a bizarre way. Dew forms at night between the thorns on their backs. The water flows to their mouths—and the lizards lap it up.

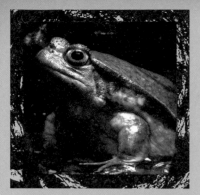

The tomato frog's red color warns predators away. It tells enemies that they may look delicious, but they are not good to eat. Tomato frogs give out a thick, sticky substance from their skins. Animals that bite them find their jaws glued together. But all tomato frogs live on Madagascar, an island off the coast of Africa. So you only need to watch out for them there.

#97 TOMATO FROGS ARE STICKY LIKE GLUE

#98 TUATARAS MOVE VERY SLOWLY

Tuataras are not like other reptiles, which often live in warm parts of the world. These lizardlike reptiles live on cold islands near New Zealand. A tuatara's body temperature is lower than that of any other reptile. Because it is so cool, the tuatara moves very slowly. It sleeps most of the day in its burrow or lying in the sun. At night it hunts for insects and spiders—slowly.

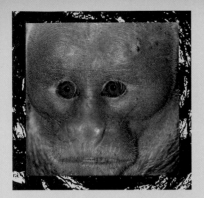

Bald, short-tailed uakari monkeys live in the forests of South America. No one knows why their faces are bright red. Some say they turn red when they get angry or excited. One thing is sure: The red color fades when uakaris are sick. A bright red face is a sign of good health.

#99 UAKARIS HAVE RED FACES

#100 UMBRELLA BIRDS CARRY "UMBRELLAS"

Umbrella birds have crowns of feathers above their heads that look like small umbrellas. These umbrellas are in place even when it's not raining! Most birds sing, chirp, whistle, or honk. But umbrella birds may be the only ones that hum. Even hummingbirds don't hum. They get their name from the whirring sound of their wings.

The viper fish has looks that can kill. Its bottom teeth are so long that they stick out of its mouth. When a viper fish spots its prey, it heads toward it at top speed with its mouth wide open. *Slam!* It smashes into the prey, stabbing it with its teeth. In a flash, the viper swallows the prey and looks for its next meal.

#101 VIPER FISH HAVE TEETH LIKE NEEDLES

INDEX

PHOTO CREDITS